USING THIS BOOK

*One of the best ways of helping children to learn to read is by reading stories to them and with them. This way they learn what **reading** is, and they will gradually come to recognise many words, and begin to read for themselves.*

First, grown-ups read the story on the left-hand pages aloud to the child.

You can reread the story as often as the child enjoys hearing it. Talk about the pictures as you go.

Later the child is encouraged to read the words under the pictures on the right-hand page.

Further suggestions for helping your child to read are given in the Parent/Teacher booklet.

British Library Cataloguing in Publication Data

McCullagh, Sheila K.
    Poor Peter Tall. —(Puddle Lane).
    I. Title   II. Rowe, Gavin   III. Series
    823'.914[J]   PZ7
    ISBN 0-7214-1055-3

First edition

Published by Ladybird Books Ltd Loughborough Leicestershire UK
Ladybird Books Inc Lewiston Maine 04240 USA

Printed in England

Poor
Peter Tall

written by SHEILA McCULLAGH
illustrated by GAVIN ROWE

This book belongs to:

Ladybird Books

One Saturday morning, Tim Catchamouse
started out to explore Puddle Lane.
He went under the gate
of the Magician's garden,
and on down the lane.
He was just going past Mr Puffle's house,
when he saw the big dog
lying fast asleep in the sunshine.

Tim saw
the big dog.

There was a long ladder leaning
up against Mr Puffle's house.
(Mr Puffle had been cleaning out his gutters.)
Tim climbed up the ladder, and
started to go back towards
the Magician's garden,
jumping from roof to roof,
until he came to Peter Tall's house.
And then there was no other roof
to jump on to.
Tim looked down.
The wall of the Magician's garden
looked a long way below.

Tim looked down.

Tim was just going to go back
to Mr Puffle's ladder, when
Mr Puffle came out of his door,
picked up his ladder, and
took it away down the lane.
Tim looked all around.
He couldn't see any way down.
"Miaow!" cried Tim. "Miaow!"
He mewed as loudly as he could,
hoping the Magician would hear him.

"Miaow!" cried Tim.
"Miaow!"

The Magician was out,
but Peter Tall heard Tim mew.
He opened his front door,
and looked out.
He couldn't see anyone,
so he stepped out into Puddle Lane.
"Miaow!" cried Tim, looking down
over the edge of the roof.

Peter Tall
opened his door.

Peter Tall looked up, and saw Tim.

"Poor little cat!" he said.

"I must get you down."

Peter Tall was a kind man,

but he wasn't very good

at doing things.

That wouldn't have mattered,

if he had let other people help him.

But he wouldn't.

He wanted to do everything himself.

And Peter Tall had had a bad week.

Peter Tall looked up
and saw Tim.

On Monday, he had found a crack
in a pane of glass
in one of his top windows.
Mr Puffle had offered
to mend it for him, but
Peter Tall wanted to mend it himself.

Monday

He had got out his ladder,
and put in a new pane.
But as he climbed down the ladder,
he slipped, and his foot hit
the middle window.
The glass broke.
Peter hadn't any more glass
to mend that window, so
he had to cover the hole
with a piece of cardboard.

Peter's foot
hit the window.

On Tuesday,
Peter had baked an apple pie.
He took it next door,
to give to old Mrs Winter.
(Old Mrs Winter had a very bad cold,
and couldn't go out shopping.)
Peter Tall really was a **very** kind man.

Tuesday

But as old Mrs Winter opened her door,
Peter Tall slipped on the steps,
and tossed the apple pie
into the house, right over her head.
So poor Mrs Winter
had no apple pie.
She had to clean it all up
off her best carpet.

Old Mrs Winter
opened the door.

On Wednesday, Peter Tall
had seen Mr Puffle's ladder
leaning up against Mr Puffle's house.
Peter Tall thought that
Mr Puffle must have forgotten
to put the ladder away.
So he took it round
to Mr Puffle's back garden,
and left it lying there.

Wednesday

But Mr Puffle was up
on the roof of his house,
fixing a chimney which was loose. And
when he wanted to climb down again,
the ladder had gone.
Mr Puffle was **very** cross.
It was a long time before
Peter Tall heard his shouts for help,
and brought the ladder back for him.

Mr Puffle was up
on the roof.

On Thursday, Peter Tall had gone
to see old Mr Gotobed.
Mr Gotobed had a bad cold, too.
Mr Gotobed stayed in bed and
Peter went in to make him
a cup of tea.
But he forgot to fill the kettle
before he put it on the fire,
and he burnt a big hole in it.
Mr Gotobed sighed a deep sigh,
and said that he would make
his tea himself, next time.

Thursday

On Friday, Peter had gone to the market.
It was a very wet day, and
Puddle Lane was full of puddles.
As he was coming home
with a basket full of cheese and cakes,
Peter slipped on a wet stone, and
sat down right in the middle
of a very big puddle.
(The cheese and cakes fell out
of the basket, all over the lane,
and the Wideawake Mice
spent a very busy night,
taking all the bits of cheese and cake
back to their home in the hollow tree.)

Friday

And now it was Saturday morning,
and Tim Catchamouse
was up on Peter Tall's roof.
As Peter came back with his ladder,
Sarah and Davy came out
of their front door, into Puddle Lane.
"What are you doing?" asked Sarah.

"I'm going to rescue
that poor little cat," said Peter Tall.
He put the ladder against the roof.
"Is that ladder safe?" asked Sarah.
"It looks a bit rickety."

"Of course it's safe," said Peter Tall.

Saturday

He was half-way up,
when the ladder broke.
Peter Tall fell down into Puddle Lane
with a great CRASH!
And the broken ladder
fell on top of him!

Peter Tall fell down
into Puddle Lane.

Sarah and Davy ran to help him.
Mr Gotobed heard the crash, and
ran out of his house.
Poor Peter Tall was covered in bruises,
but he wasn't badly hurt.
Sarah and Davy helped him
to get to his feet.
"You need to sit down, and
have a cup of tea,"
said old Mr Gotobed.
"Come over to my house, and
I'll put the saucepan on to boil."

Mr Gotobed ran
out of his house.

Sarah and Davy helped Peter Tall
to limp across the lane
to Mr Gotobed's house.
Then they went back to clear up
the broken bits of ladder.
Davy had just picked up a long bit,
when they heard a mew.
They looked up, and saw
Tim Catchamouse looking down
over the edge of the roof.

Sarah and Davy
looked up.
They saw
Tim Catchamouse.

"I know what we can do,"
said Davy. "Give me a hand with this."
Sarah and Davy took
the long piece of ladder
over to their own house, and
set it up against a top windowsill.
"Let's go inside and watch," said Davy.
"If we keep very quiet,
the little cat won't be frightened."

Sarah and Davy
set up the ladder.

Tim Catchamouse looked down
into Puddle Lane.
There was no one there.
He saw the broken piece of ladder.
He jumped down on to
old Mrs Winter's roof, and
then on to Sarah and Davy's house.
He ran down the roof, and
climbed down the broken ladder.
He ran safely back
to the Magician's garden, and
told Pegs all about his adventures.

Tim and Pegs

Do you know the days of the week?

Monday

Tuesday

Wednesday

Thursday

Friday

Saturday

What do you think Peter Tall did on

Sunday?

Notes for the parent/teacher

When you have finished the story, go through the book again, looking at the pictures and discussing the story with the child.

Point to the captions below the pictures, and encourage the child to read them, reading them aloud yourself, if she* is not sure of a word.

Print the names of the days of the week on separate pieces of cardboard, and encourage her to put one up each day, so that she learns to recognise the words.

Read the story again as often as the child likes hearing it. The more opportunities she has of looking at illustrations and reading with you, the more she will come to recognise words.

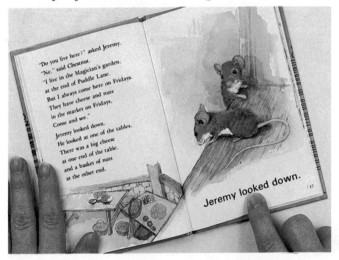

"Do you live here?" asked Jeremy.
"No," said Chestnut.
"I live in the Magician's garden,
at the end of Puddle Lane.
But I always come here on Fridays.
They have cheese and nuts
in the market on Fridays.
Come and see."
Jeremy looked down.
He looked at one of the tables.
There was a big cheese
at one end of the table,
and a basket of nuts
at the other end.

Jeremy looked down.

*Footnote: In order to avoid the continual "he or she", "him or her", the child is referred to in this book as "she". However, the stories are equally appropriate to boys and girls.

There are several books at this Stage about the same characters. All the books at each Stage are separate stories and are written at the same reading level.
Here are some other books from Stage 1.

Stage 1

1 Tim Catchamouse
2 Tessa and the Magician
3 The magic box
7 The flying saucer
8 Two green ears
9 The tale of a tail

*from
Tim Catchamouse*

*from
The magic box*